FOSSILS

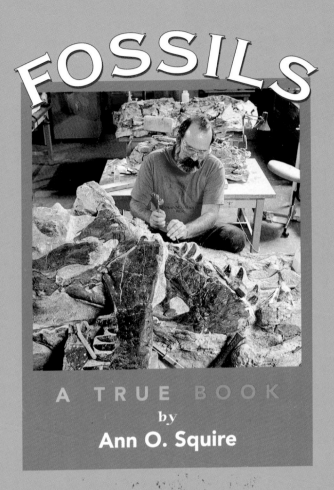

A TRUE BOOK

by

Ann O. Squire

Children's Press®

A Division of Scholastic Inc.

New York Toronto London Auckland Sydney
Mexico City New Delhi Hong Kong
Danbury, Connecticut

Skull of a
Tyrannosaurus rex

Reading and Content
Consultant
Jan Jenner

Author's Dedication
To my daughter, Emma

*The photograph on the cover
shows a fish fossil. The
photograph on the title page
shows a paleontologist
chipping a fossil out of a rock.*

Library of Congress Cataloging-in-Publication Data

Squire, Ann.
    Fossils / by Ann O. Squire.
        p.   cm. – (True Books)
    Includes index.
    Summary: An introduction to fossils, discussing the different types,
where they are found, and how they are made.
    ISBN 0-516-22504-9 (lib. bdg.)   0-516-26982-8 (pbk.)
    1. Fossils—Juvenile literature. [1. Fossils.] I. Title. II Series
QE714.5 S65 2002
560—dc21   2001005758

Contents

Tyrannosaurus rex (above) and a saber-toothed cat (left)

Clues to the Past

Have you ever seen a picture of a saber-toothed cat? What about an armor-plated stegosaurus or a fierce Tyrannosaurus rex? "Of course!" you'd answer. "Everyone knows what those animals looked like." But did you ever wonder *how* we know? After all, these three animals lived during prehistoric times.

All of them have been extinct
for thousands, or even millions,
of years.

Because these animals are no
longer alive, scientists must
look at fossils to learn how they
looked and acted. Fossils are
the remains, or traces, of animals and plants that have been
preserved in Earth's crust.
Fossils can be actual remains,
such as petrified bones, teeth,
or shells. Fossils can also be
traces of animals, such as foot-
prints, burrows, or molds of an

This fossil of a seed fern (top left) is more than 170 million years old. These fossilized bones (top right) make up the hind foot of a sauropod. Dinosaur prints are much, much larger than our own (bottom).

animal's body. A fossil can even be something the animal left behind—lumpy coprolites are actually the fossilized droppings of animals that lived long ago.

The youngest fossils that have been found are remains of animals preserved during the last ice age, about 10,000 years ago. The oldest are traces of blue-green algae (tiny plants) that lived more than 3 *billion* years ago.

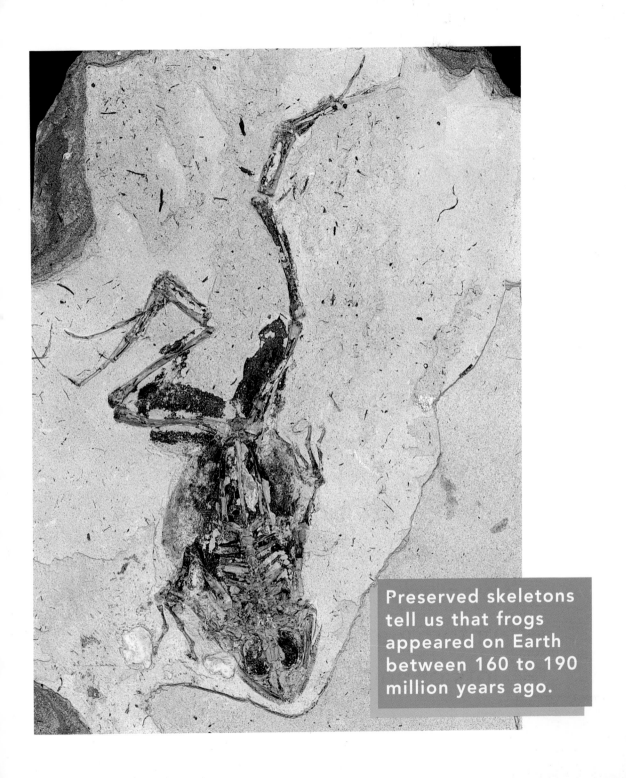

Preserved skeletons tell us that frogs appeared on Earth between 160 to 190 million years ago.

How Are Fossils Created?

Dinosaur fossils have told us a lot about how these animals lived millions of years ago. Do you think that we can learn about every prehistoric animal by studying fossils? The answer, unfortunately, is no because lots of animals never even turn

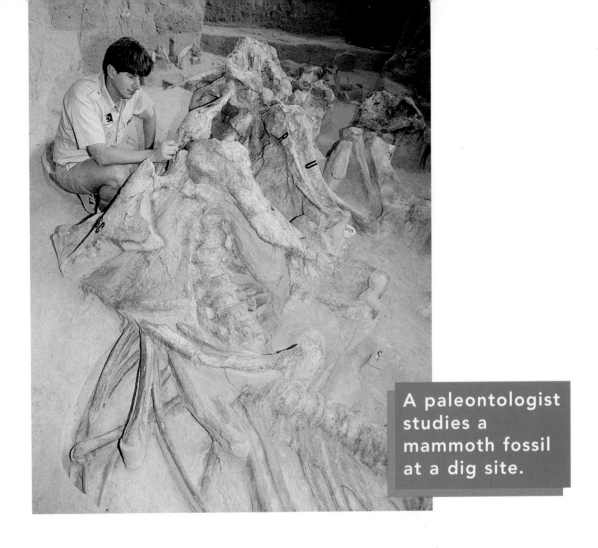

A paleontologist studies a mammoth fossil at a dig site.

into fossils. Think about what paleontologists (scientists who study fossils) usually dig up: bones. Animals without bones,

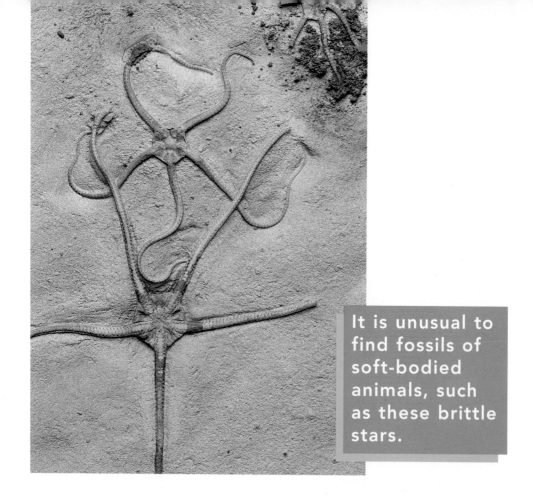

shells, or other hard parts usually don't become fossils. So there are probably many prehistoric worms, jellyfish, octopuses, and other soft-bodied animals that we will never know about because they never left any fossil remains.

Animals with bones don't always become fossils, either. After an animal dies, it usually decomposes (rots) or is eaten by another animal. Its bones are scattered all around. They may even be completely destroyed, so that no trace of the animal is left. In order to become a fossil, an animal's body must be covered up very

This is a fossil of a sea scorpion. These animals became extinct about 200 million years ago.

quickly by mud, sand, or another material. This is most likely to happen underwater. For this reason, most fossils are found in places that were once covered by oceans.

Let's imagine how a fossil fish might be created and dis-covered millions of years later. A fish dies and sinks to the bottom of the ocean. Before another animal has a chance to eat it, the fish's body is cov-ered by a layer of sand. As time goes by, more and more layers of sand and mud cover the fish. Each new layer press-es down on the deeper layers. After many, many years, the sand is squeezed so much that it turns to rock, with the bones of the fish trapped inside. Water seeping through the rock may dissolve the minerals in the bones, and replace them with other, harder minerals. This creates a petrified fossil (petrified means "turned to stone").

Over millions of years, the land changes. The sea dries up and earthquakes bring deep layers of rock to the surface. An amateur paleontologist (maybe even you!) is chipping away at a

These fish were trapped between layers of sand that eventually turned to stone.

rocky cliff and suddenly sees a perfect fossilized skeleton of a fish that has been encased in the rock for millions of years.

Where Do Fossils Come From?

Paleontologists have unearthed fossils all over the world—even north of the Arctic Circle and near the South Pole. No matter where on Earth you live, the chances are good that fossils have been found nearby. If you live

These paleontologists are uncovering a giant mastodon near Hemet, California.

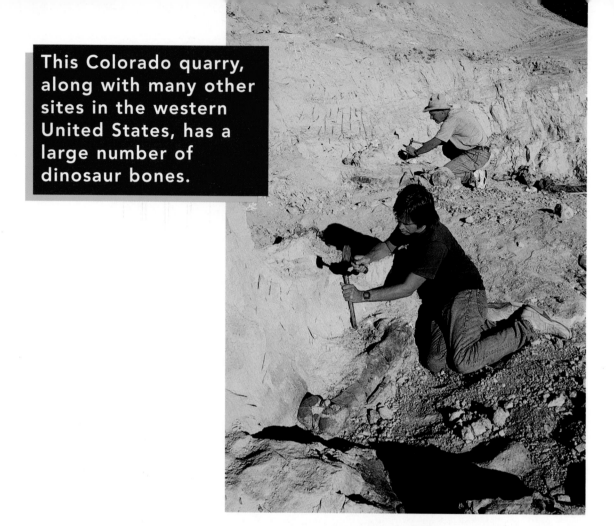

This Colorado quarry, along with many other sites in the western United States, has a large number of dinosaur bones.

in the central or western part of the United States or Canada, you're really in luck— lots of dinosaurs dating back to the Jurassic and Cretaceous periods (180 million to 65 million years ago) have been found right in your backyard.

In Chapter 2, we learned that most fossils are created when many layers of mud, sand, and other sediment build up.

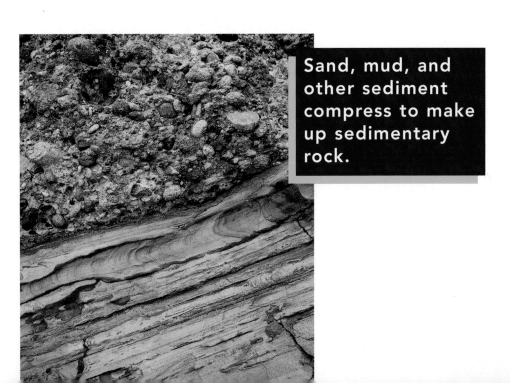

Sand, mud, and other sediment compress to make up sedimentary rock.

The rocks that are formed by these many layers are called sedimentary rocks. It is in sedimentary rocks that most (but not all) fossils are found.

It's easy to tell if a rock or a cliff or the side of a hill is made up of sedimentary rock. Just look for the crosswise layers, called strata. Each layer comes from mud, sand, clay, or other sediment that built up and turned to stone millions of years ago.

Sedimentary rock has many
horizontal layers called strata.

One of the most spectacular sedimentary rocks you'll ever see is the Grand Canyon, in Arizona. Here, the Colorado River has sliced through Earth's crust, almost like slicing down through a many-layered cake. The layers near the top of the canyon are the youngest, while those near the bottom are close to 2 billion years old. Different kinds of fossils are found at different levels. The limestone rocks near the top

The Colorado River Canyon in Grand Canyon National Park has many layers of strata that have been exposed by the river's erosion.

are about 200 million years old. These contain fossils of insects, reptiles, and ferns. Farther down, in rocks about 400 million

The tops of the canyon walls in Grand Canyon National Park are made of limestone, and are about 200 million years old.

years old, scientists have found fossils of prehistoric armored fish. At the very bottom, where the rocks are the oldest, there are no signs of life at all.

Different Eras, Different Animals

Knowing that fossils from deep layers of rock are older than fossils found nearer to the surface helps paleontologists figure out what animals lived when. Let's take a look at what life was like thousands, millions, and hundreds of millions of years ago.

People look at dinosaur bones at a dig site in Peru.

Scientists believe that Earth is 4 billion years old. But it was not until about 570 million years ago that many forms of life began to appear. From this time until about 240 million years ago is called the Paleozoic era. Primitive animals such as sponges, worms, and snails were common at the beginning of this era. Toward the middle of the Paleozoic era (about 400 million

Worms first appeared on Earth during the Paleozoic era.

This is a horseshoe crab fossil. Shellfish also appeared during the Paleozoic era.

years ago), fish first appeared. Then came shellfish, amphibians, and insects, including a giant dragonfly whose wingspan measured nearly 3 feet (1 meter). By the end of the Paleozoic era, reptiles had appeared.

During the next era, called the Mesozoic, reptiles overshadowed all other animals, including mammals. In fact, this era, which lasted from 240 million to 63 million years ago, is often called the Age of Reptiles. It was during this time that triceratops,

The triceratops appeared in the Mesozoic era, which is also known as the Age of Reptiles.

tyrannosaurus, and other dinosaurs roamed Earth. But by the end of the Mesozoic era, all the dinosaurs had become extinct.

The last era, from 65 million years ago up until the present day, is called the Cenozoic. It is also known as the Age of Mammals, since mammals replaced the ruling reptiles of the Mesozoic era. Giant rhino-like animals, mastodons, and saber-toothed cats were some

Mastodons lived during the Age of Mammals in the Cenozoic era.

of the mammals that lived during this era. Amazingly, everything we know about life on Earth for the past 600 million years has been discovered by studying fossils!

Trapped!

Most fossils occur when an animal or a plant is covered by layers of sediment, which later turn to rock. But not every fossil is created that way. In some cases, prehistoric animals were trapped, and preserved, in ice, sticky tree sap, or tar.

These trilobite fossils formed when they were covered by sediment on the ocean floor.

Amber, a brown material used to make jewelry, is actually fossilized sap from trees that lived millions of years ago. Sometimes insects, spiders, or even small lizards accidentally stumbled into the goo and got

These prehistoric insects became trapped in amber and it hardened around them.

stuck. When the sap hardened, these animals were trapped forever. Scientists have found lumps of amber containing perfectly preserved insects and lizards that lived 40 million years ago!

Larger animals sometimes got stuck in pools of tar that oozed up through cracks in Earth's crust. In Los Angeles, California, towering skyscrapers have replaced the grassy plains that existed during the last ice age, tens of thousands of years

This animal sculpture at the La Brea Tar Pits shows how animals got stuck in the gooey substance.

ago. At that time, many animals, such as lions, camels, giant sloths, mastodons, wolves, and saber-toothed cats roamed the wild lands of what is now southern California.

How do scientists know this? In the early 1900s, people noticed that the hardened tar contained bones. When paleontologists looked at the bones, they realized that they were those of a giant ground sloth that had lived thousands of years ago. Later they unearthed

This is a fossil of a saber-toothed cat skull (above). The species is extinct today. Wolves (right) were around at the time of the last ice age, and the species still exists in California today.

the bones of many other animals. Some of them, like the American lion and the saber-toothed cat, are now extinct. Others, such as the California mole and the gray wolf, still live in California.

Paleontologists believe
that animals sometimes stumbled into the pools of tar
(during the summer, when the

tar was very soft) and got stuck. The helpless animals probably attracted predators, such as lions and wolves, which also became trapped and died. As the bones became soaked with tar, they sank to the bottom of the pool. There they were preserved, awaiting the paleontologists who would one day dig them up and use them to solve the mystery of what life on Earth was like in prehistoric times.

Dinosaur Days

Cartoons often show early humans, or "cavemen," sharing Earth with giant dinosaurs. Did this really happen? No. It is true that dinosaurs and early humans both lived in prehistoric times, but they didn't live at the same time. When humans appeared on Earth, dinosaurs had been extinct for about 65 million years.

To Find Out More

Here are some additional resources to help you learn more about fossils:

 **Books**

Dixon, Douglas. **Carnivores.** Gareth Stevens, 2001.

Parker, Steve, Murray Weston, and Jane Parker. **Collecting Fossils: Hold Prehistory in the Palm of Your Hand.** Sterling Publications, 1998.

Pirolta, Saviour. **Fossils and Bones.** Raintree, Steck Vaughn, 1997.

Thompson, Sharon Elaine. **Death Trap: The Story of the La Brea Tar Pits.** Lerner Publications, 1994.

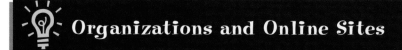

Organizations and Online Sites

The Denver Museum of Nature and Science
www.dmnh.org

Site features a Colossal Fossil Adventure learning game, as well as general information on fossils and paleontology.

The National Science Museum
www.geo.nsf.gov/ear/ earkids.htm

Many links to helpful earth science sites for kids.

The La Brea Tar Pits
Los Angeles, California.
www.tarpits.org

Lots of information about fossils and about animals and plants that lived during the last ice age.

The San Diego Natural History Museum
www.sdnhm.org/kids/fossils

Lots of great photographs and information on where to find and view fossils. Dinosaur facts and games are also included.

Important Words

amber a hard, yellow-brown material used in making jewelry. Amber is the fossilized sap of trees that lived millions of years ago.

fossil the remains of an animal or a plant that lived long ago

paleontologist a scientist who studies fossils to learn about life during prehistoric times

petrified something that has been turned into stone or a stonelike substance

prehistoric the time before written history

sedimentary rock rock that is formed from many layers of sand, mud, or other sediment that builds up over many years

strata layers

Index

Meet the Author

Ann O. Squire has a Ph.D. in animal behavior. Before becoming a writer, she studied African electric fish, rats, and other animals. Dr. Squire has written many books on animals, animal behavior, and other natural-science topics. Her most recent books for Children's Press include *Animal Babies*, *Seashells*, *Gemstones*, and *Growing Crystals*. She lives with her children, Emma and Evan, in Bedford, New York.